# Space travel timeline

Here are some highlights of our exploration of space with manned and unmanned spacecraft. Where will we go in the future?

## International Space Station

The ISS is the largest structure in space. It has been occupied since November 2000.

## Hubble Space Telescope (HST)

Launched in 1990, Hubble was the first major optical telescope in space. It has taken amazing photos of the universe.

## Curiosity rover

This unmanned spacecraft has explored the surface of Mars since August 2012.

Seven cameras on this mast provide stunning images and help navigate.

**The first ISS crew**

| 1986 | 1990 | 2000 | 2005 | 2010 | 2012 | 2018 |

## Mir Space Station

Mir was launched in 1986. Thirty-nine missions flew to it, up to June 2000.

## SpaceX

This is the first private company to produce reusable rocket launchers and spacecraft.

## Cassini-Huygens

Launched in 1997, it took over seven years to reach Saturn, exploring there until 2017.

## Transiting Exoplanet Survey Satellite

TESS will cover the whole sky over two years, looking for planets orbiting other stars.

The Radio and Plasma Wave Spectrometer measured radio signals from Saturn.

Things to find out:

# DKfindout!

# Space Travel

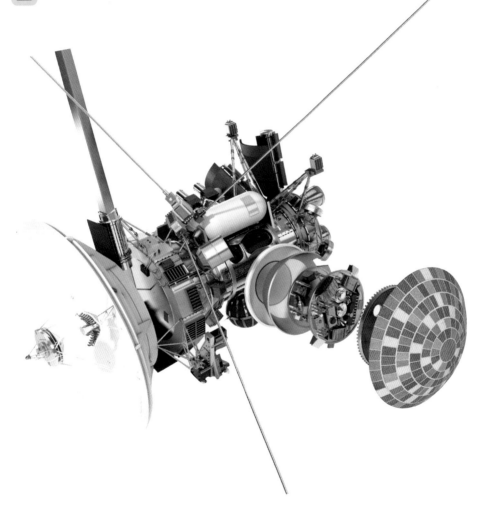

Author: Jerry Stone
Consultant: Peter Bond

**Senior editor** Carrie Love
**Editor** Kritika Gupta
**US editor** Allison Singer
**Designer** Bettina Myklebust Stovne
**Art editor** Shubham Rohatgi
**DTP designers** Dheeraj Singh, Mohd Rizwan
**Picture researcher** Sakshi Saluja
**Jacket co-ordinator** Francesca Young
**Jacket designer** Suzena Sengupta
**Managing editors** Laura Gilbert, Monica Saigal
**Deputy managing art editor** Ivy Sengupta
**Managing art editor** Diane Peyton Jones
**Senior producer, pre-production** Tony Phipps
**Senior producer** Isabell Schart
**Delhi team head** Malavika Talukder
**Creative director** Helen Senior
**Publishing director** Sarah Larter
**Educational consultant** Jacqueline Harris

**This book is dedicated to** Phoebe

First American Edition, 2019
Published in the United States by DK Publishing
345 Hudson Street, New York, New York 10014

Copyright © 2019 Dorling Kindersley Limited
DK, a Division of Penguin Random House LLC
19 20 21 22 23 10 9 8 7 6 5 4 3 2 1
001–311565–Feb/2019

A catalog record for this book
is available from the Library of Congress.
ISBN: 978-1-4654-7931-0 (Flexibound)
ISBN: 978-1-4654-7932-7 (Hardcover)

DK books are available at special discounts when purchased in bulk for sales
promotions, premiums, fund-raising, or educational use. For details, contact: DK
Publishing Special Markets, 345 Hudson Street, New York, New York 10014
SpecialSales@dk.com

Printed and bound in China.

A WORLD OF IDEAS:
SEE ALL THERE IS TO KNOW

www.dk.com

# Contents

**4** What is space?

**6** Early astronomers

**8** Space pioneers

**10** The Space Race

**12** Space programs

**14** Space shuttle

**16** Shuttle service

**18** Rockets

**20** Spaceplanes

**22** Mission Control

**24** Mission to the moon

Chang'e 2

The Apollo 11 crew

Sojourner

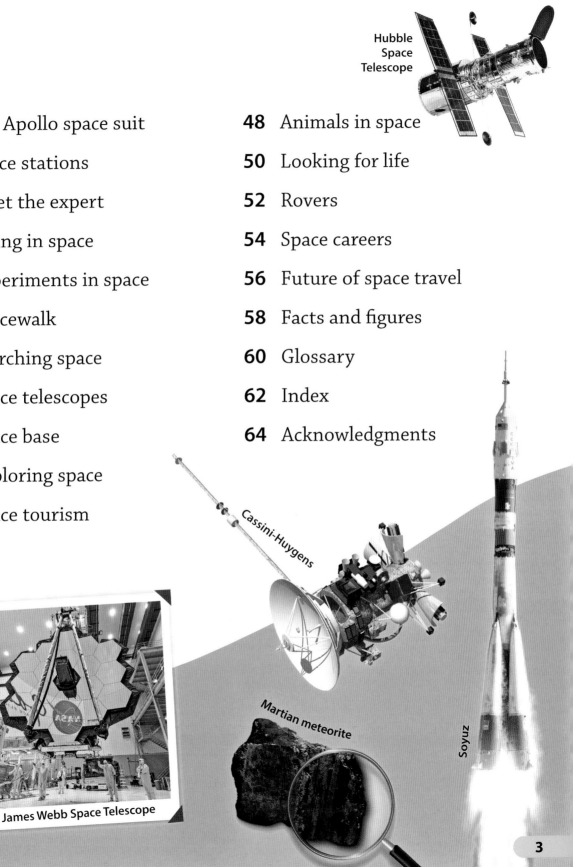

Hubble
Space
Telescope

26 The Apollo space suit

28 Space stations

30 Meet the expert

32 Living in space

34 Experiments in space

36 Spacewalk

38 Searching space

40 Space telescopes

42 Space base

44 Exploring space

46 Space tourism

48 Animals in space

50 Looking for life

52 Rovers

54 Space careers

56 Future of space travel

58 Facts and figures

60 Glossary

62 Index

64 Acknowledgments

Cassini-Huygens

Martian meteorite

Soyuz

James Webb Space Telescope

# What is space?

We live on planet Earth, one of eight main planets that orbit the sun—our local star. Together with moons, rocky lumps called asteroids, and icy objects called comets, these make up our solar system. The solar system is part of a galaxy (a massive collection of stars) called the Milky Way. There may be about two trillion galaxies in the universe.

**Galaxies**
Galaxies vary in size and shape. The galaxy shown here is a spiral galaxy, which spins around, like a giant whirlpool.

# What is in space?

Space contains all the planets, moons, stars, and galaxies, along with other things, such as star clusters (groups of stars) and nebulas (huge clouds of gas and dust). Space also contains dust, gas, and radiation.

The Cat's Paw and Lobster Nebulas

**Stars and nebulas**
Stars are giant shining globes of gas. There are about 250 billion stars in the Milky Way. In the two nebulas shown here, new stars are forming.

## Why is space black?

To answer this, let's look at why our daytime sky is blue. This is because sunlight hits tiny things called molecules in the Earth's air and scatters them, causing the sky to look blue. In space, there is no air, so therefore it looks black.

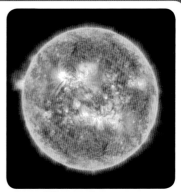

The sun in space

Planets in space

Meteor shower

**Planets and moons**
We have eight main planets and five dwarf (small) planets in our solar system. Most have one or more moons orbiting them.

**Comets, asteroids, and meteors**
There are millions of icy comets and rocky asteroids. Meteors are mainly tiny grains of dust.

# Early astronomers

Astronomy is the study of space, including stars and planets. At first, people believed in the Earth was at the center of the universe (the Geocentric system). Over time, people realized that planets orbited the sun (the Heliocentric system). The invention of the telescope helped us better understand the universe.

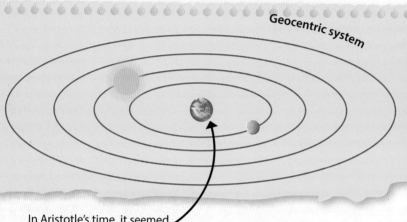

Geocentric system

In Aristotle's time, it seemed that the sun, the moon, and stars all circled the Earth.

### Ptolemy

Living around 1,800 years ago, Ptolemy produced tables that could be used to predict the positions of the sun, the moon, and stars. He thought, incorrectly, that everything moved in perfect circles.

### Aristotle

About 2,300 years ago, Aristotle believed the Earth was at the center of everything. He thought that other objects revolved around the Earth, because this is what appeared to happen when watching them in the sky.

**Astronomy is the oldest science.**

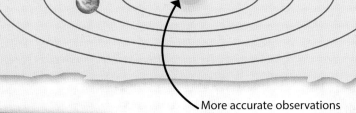

Heliocentric system

More accurate observations led us to realize that all the planets actually go around the sun.

## Copernicus

In 1543, Nicolaus Copernicus changed our view of the planets by suggesting that they all orbit the sun. This went against the old idea that the Earth was the center of everything.

Galileo made a refracting telescope, which means it used lenses. His early telescopes were much smaller than this one.

## Galileo

After the telescope was invented in 1609, Italian scientist Galileo Galilei built one himself and observed the four main moons of Jupiter. Here were objects that clearly did not orbit the Earth. He also observed other objects, including the sun and the moon.

# Space pioneers

The first human space flight was by Russian cosmonaut (astronaut) Yuri Gagarin in 1961. Since then, many other men and women have blazed a trail through space. Today, April 12 is celebrated around the world as "Yuri's Night," honoring achievements in space exploration.

## YURI GAGARIN

On April 12, 1961, Russian cosmonaut Yuri Gagarin made a single orbit around Earth in Vostok 1. This meant that the Soviet Union (Russia) had beaten its rival, the USA, with putting a human in space.

## ALEXEI LEONOV

In 1965, Leonov became the first person to conduct an Extra Vehicular Activity (EVA)—a "spacewalk." This is when astronauts go outside their spacecraft. Leonov spent 12 minutes outside Voskhod 2.

## THE APOLLO 11 CREW

Commander of Apollo 11, Neil Armstrong was the first person in history to walk on the surface of another world. He landed the Lunar Module *Eagle* on the moon with Edwin "Buzz" Aldrin on July 20, 1969. Michael Collins stayed in orbit around the moon.

## VALENTINA TERESHKOVA

Two years after Gagarin's flight, Russia launched the first female cosmonaut in June 1963. She spent almost three days orbiting the Earth in Vostok 6. The next woman in space would not fly until 1982!

## PEGGY WHITSON

Whitson holds the record for the most time spent in space by a woman, and by any American astronaut, at 665 days. In 2007, she became the first female commander of the ISS.

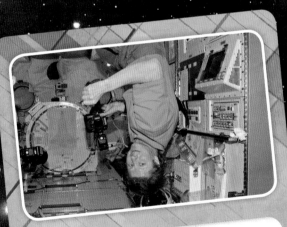

## GENNADY PADALKA

The Russian cosmonaut Gennady Padalka made five space flights: one to the Russian space station (Mir) and four to the International Space Station (ISS). He holds the record for the most total time spent in space—878 days.

# The Space Race

The USA planned to launch a satellite into orbit around Earth in 1957. However, they were beaten by the launch of the Russian satellite, Sputnik 1 on October 4, 1957. The USA wanted to catch up, and so the Space Race between these two powerful nations was born.

**Mercury 7**
April 9, 1959: The USA announced its Project Mercury astronauts: (Back) Shepard, Grissom, Cooper; (Front) Schirra, Slayton, Glenn, and Carpenter.

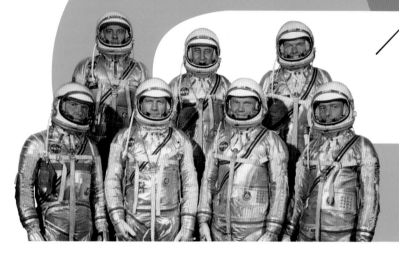

**Kennedy's 1961 speech**
May 25, 1961: President Kennedy challenged the USA to land a man on the moon before the end of the decade.

**First footprint on the moon**
Because there is no wind or rain there, an astronaut's footprint could last on the moon for millions of years.

**Man on the moon**
July 20, 1969: Neil Armstrong and Buzz Aldrin landed the Apollo 11 Lunar Module *Eagle* and then walked on the moon.

### Sputnik
October 4, 1957: Russia launched the first artificial satellite, Sputnik 1. It circled the Earth every 96 minutes.

### First American satellite
January 31, 1958: The USA's first satellite, Explorer 1, led to the discovery of the Van Allen radiation belts. These trap high energy solar particles.

The tiny Explorer 1 satellite weighed 31 lb (14 kg).

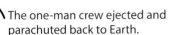

The one-man crew ejected and parachuted back to Earth.

### Vostok 1
April 12, 1961: Yuri Gagarin became the first person in space, making a single orbit of the Earth in 108 minutes.

### Lunar probe
October 6, 1959: Russia's Luna 3 flew around the moon, taking photos of its far side (the side not seen from Earth).

Luna 3's photos were picked up by the radio telescope at Britain's Jodrell Bank observatory.

In June 1965, Ed White made the first American spacewalk.

### First American in space
May 5, 1961: Alan Shepard made a suborbital space flight, and John Glenn flew into orbit on February 20, 1962.

### Project Gemini
Between March 1965 and December 1966, 10 two-man Gemini flights tried out activities needed for the moon missions to follow.

# Space programs

Until recently, space programs, or plans to explore, were carried out on behalf of government space agencies. Now private companies also run space activities, which will increase with the rise of space tourism (space travel for leisure). There are more than 70 national space agencies.

**European Space Agency (ESA)**
ESA launches satellites and space probes, and also has a team of astronauts. Its headquarters are in Paris, France.

ESA's Gaia is a space observatory designed to produce the largest and most precise 3-D catalog of space objects.

NASA's InSight was sent to Mars in 2018 to drill beneath its surface and study inside the planet.

**National Aeronautics and Space Administration (NASA)**
Created in 1958, NASA's projects include sending astronauts to the moon exploring the solar system and beyond.

**China National Space Administration (CNSA)**
Since 2003, China has sent more than 10 men and women into space. Chinese astronauts are called taikonauts.

Russia's Mission Control space center is in the city of Korolev.

**Russian space agency (Roscosmos)**
Formed in 1992 after the end of the Soviet Union, Roscosmos runs space activities for the Russian Federation.

In 2003, Yang Liwei became the first person sent into space by the Chinese space program.

The 37th launch of the very successful H-IIA rocket carried two satellites into orbit.

**Indian Space Research Organisation (ISRO)**
India has sent spacecraft to the moon and to Mars, and has launched satellites, too.

Chandrayaan-1 was India's first probe to the moon. It was launched in 2008.

**The Japan Aerospace Exploration Agency (JAXA)**
Japan has launched space telescopes and probes for space research, communications, and observations.

# Space shuttle

From 1981 to 2011, the space shuttle was the main space launch vehicle of the United States. Four Orbiters were originally built: *Columbia*, *Challenger*, *Discovery*, and *Atlantis*. *Columbia* and *Challenger* were destroyed in tragic accidents that killed their crews. *Endeavour* was built as a replacement for *Challenger*.

## External Tank

The main engines were fueled by the External Tank. This was separated after the engines were shut down. The tank broke up as it fell into the ocean.

## Solid Rocket Boosters

Two Solid Rocket Boosters helped lift the shuttle off the launch pad. They burned for two minutes, and then fell away, parachuting into the ocean, where they were picked up to be reused.

## Orbiter

The Orbiter carried a crew of up to eight people, plus cargo. This was the only part that went into orbit. When it reentered Earth's atmosphere, it glided to a runway and could be used again.

The Orbiters traveled a total of **542,398,878 miles** (872,906,379 km), carrying 355 **different people.**

## Main engines

The three main engines burned liquid hydrogen and liquid oxygen. Together, they produced nearly 1.2 million lb (540,000 kg) of thrust, taking the Orbiter from the ground to orbit in eight and a half minutes.

Discovery

United States

## Orbiter in space

Soon after lift-off, the boosters were dropped. The Orbiter's main engines continued for several more minutes. The External Tank was then discarded. Two smaller Orbital Maneuvering System (OMS) engines were used to get the Orbiter into orbit.

**Visiting Mir**
The shuttle's missions to the Russian Mir space station paved the way for building the ISS.

**3**

**2**

**The Orbiter**
The crew and cargo traveled in the Orbiter.

## Docking

Once in space, the Orbiter's cargo-bay doors were opened to allow the docking system to connect to space stations such as Mir and the ISS.

**1**

## Lift-off!

Two Solid Rocket Boosters, the External Tank, and the Orbiter were mounted on a launch pad. The tank held fuel for the Orbiter's main engines during launch. The boosters gave extra power for lift-off.

# Shuttle service

Unlike earlier spacecraft, NASA's space shuttle had reusable parts. Only the External Tank was lost. During its service life, the shuttle was used to launch satellites, space telescopes, and probes. It also helped assemble the International Space Station (ISS).

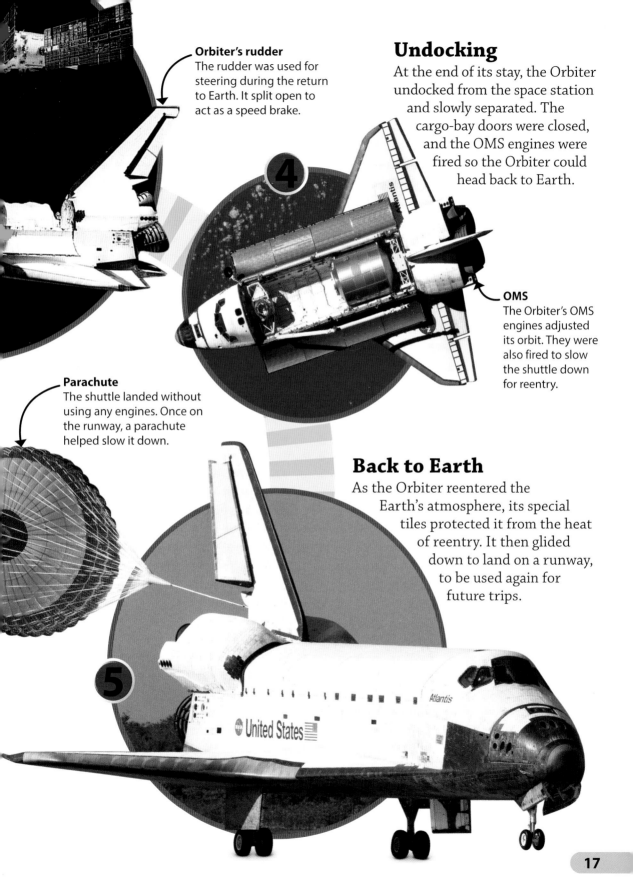

**Orbiter's rudder**
The rudder was used for steering during the return to Earth. It split open to act as a speed brake.

**④**

# Undocking

At the end of its stay, the Orbiter undocked from the space station and slowly separated. The cargo-bay doors were closed, and the OMS engines were fired so the Orbiter could head back to Earth.

**OMS**
The Orbiter's OMS engines adjusted its orbit. They were also fired to slow the shuttle down for reentry.

**Parachute**
The shuttle landed without using any engines. Once on the runway, a parachute helped slow it down.

# Back to Earth

As the Orbiter reentered the Earth's atmosphere, its special tiles protected it from the heat of reentry. It then glided down to land on a runway, to be used again for future trips.

**⑤**

Atlantis

United States

# Rockets

A rocket is a vehicle, usually tube-shaped, with powerful engines that can blast it high into the sky. To reach orbit, rockets have more than one stage, or section. As each stage uses up its fuel, it is discarded. Some types of rocket made recently can be reused.

A Falcon 9 being launched from Vandenberg Air Force Base in California

The Long March 2F was first launched in November 1999.

## Falcon

In September 2008, a Falcon 1, made by SpaceX, became the first privately funded rocket to orbit the Earth. Later models, the Falcon 9 and Falcon Heavy rockets, can reuse their first stages. This makes the cost of launches much cheaper.

## Long March 2F

This is the rocket that China has used to launch its two Tiangong space stations and the manned Shenzou spacecraft. It is a two-stage rocket, 203 ft (62 m) tall, and it is launched from the Jiuquan Satellite Launch Center.

## Saturn V rocket

The biggest and most powerful rocket ever to launch people into space was the Saturn V. It was 363 ft (110 m) high. Between December 1968 and December 1972, it carried Apollo astronauts to the moon's orbit.

Saturn V rocket

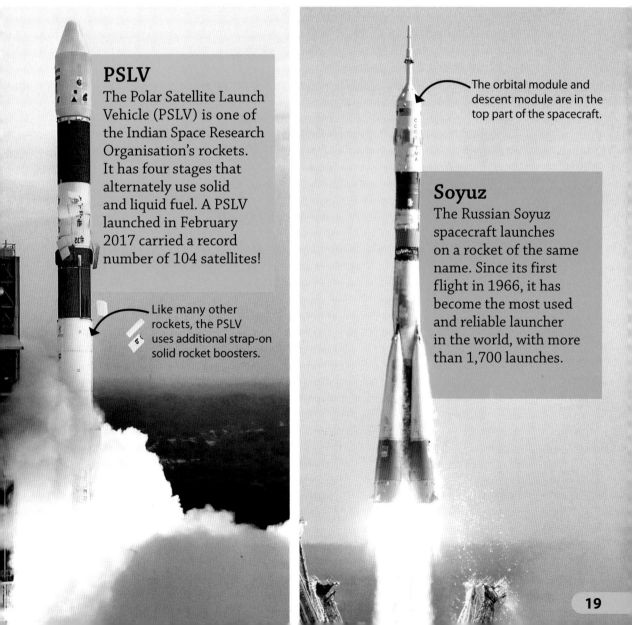

### PSLV

The Polar Satellite Launch Vehicle (PSLV) is one of the Indian Space Research Organisation's rockets. It has four stages that alternately use solid and liquid fuel. A PSLV launched in February 2017 carried a record number of 104 satellites!

Like many other rockets, the PSLV uses additional strap-on solid rocket boosters.

The orbital module and descent module are in the top part of the spacecraft.

### Soyuz

The Russian Soyuz spacecraft launches on a rocket of the same name. Since its first flight in 1966, it has become the most used and reliable launcher in the world, with more than 1,700 launches.

# Spaceplanes

Unlike rockets that launch vertically, most spaceplanes take off horizontally. Spaceplanes all land horizontally on a runway, unlike spacecraft, such as Apollo. Spaceplanes can fly many times, which is one of their major features. A space flight is when a vehicle reaches space at 62 miles (100 km) above sea level.

## Eugen Sänger

Sänger was a spaceplane pioneer. Born in 1905, he came up with the idea of a craft that would be launched on a rocket sled and which could make suborbital flights. He also designed a two-part orbital spaceplane. His work greatly influenced later designs.

## North American X-15

This is a rocket-powered aircraft carried by a B-52 bomber. Two flights by Joe Walker in July and August 1963 are considered space flights because they went above 62 miles (100 km).

## Boeing X-37B

Launched vertically, the X-37B is an unmanned vehicle. It is operated by the United States Department of Defense. Full details of its space flights are not available to the public.

## SpaceShipOne

In 2004, SpaceShipOne made two space flights within two weeks, winning the $10 million Ansari X-Prize. SpaceShipOne is launched from a carrier aircraft using its rocket motor.

## Skylon

Skylon is designed to be a spaceplane that can fly into orbit using an engine that first starts as a jet before working as a rocket. This will be possible due to the revolutionary SABRE engine.

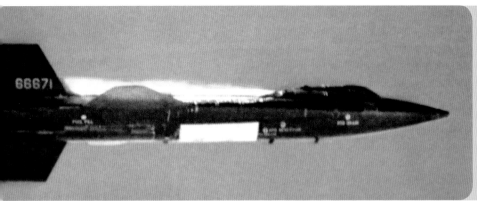

SpaceShipOne was carried by White Knight One. The larger SpaceShipTwo, carried by White Knight Two, is designed to carry up to six space tourists.

Designed to operate unmanned, Skylon could carry 12 tons (11 metric tons) to the ISS—45 percent more than a reusable Falcon 9. Test flights could take place by 2025.

Mach 1 is equivalent to the speed of sound, Mach 2 is twice the speed of sound, and so on. The X-15 holds the record for the fastest manned, powered aircraft at Mach 6.7, piloted by William Knight in 1967.

There are two X-37B craft, each carrying out long-duration missions of up to two years in orbit. They land automatically after returning from orbit.

# Mission Control

Space flights, both manned and unmanned, are controled and monitored from a mission control center, where a team of people help run the flight. There are various centers around the world. The most famous one is at the Johnson Space Center in Houston, Texas.

FLIGHT DIRECTOR

2

EVA

4

BME

5

**1**

**CAPCOM**

**3**

SPARTAN

ISO

OPS PLANNER

SURGEON

**6**

## KEY

**1** **Display screens** Screens at the front of the room that show the spacecraft's flight path, its status, and TV views from space.

**2** **Flight director** Responsible for control of the mission and for any actions needed for crew safety and mission success.

**3** **Spacecraft communicator** An astronaut who provides all of the voice communications between the ground and the spacecraft crew. Also called "CAPCOM," or capsule communicator.

**4** **Extra Vehicular Activity (EVA) control** Responsible for all space suit and spacewalking related tasks, equipment, and plans when there is EVA.

**5** **Biomedical engineer (BME)** Provides 24-hour health care support for the crew aboard the spacecraft.

**6** **Flight surgeon** Monitors the crew's health, directs all of the operational medical activities, and advises the flight director.

# Mission to the moon

People dreamed of flying to the moon for many years. In the summer of 1969, just eight years after President Kennedy's challenge, Neil Armstrong and Edwin "Buzz" Aldrin became the first humans to walk on the moon.

## Apollo 11

On July 20, 1969, Armstrong and Aldrin landed their Lunar Module *Eagle*. Third crew member, Michael Collins, orbited the moon overhead in the Command Module *Columbia*.

**Armstrong and Aldrin explored the surface of the moon for two and a half hours.**

**WOW!**

The **Apollo missions** brought back **842 lb (382 kg)** of **rock and soil** from the moon.

They set up experiments on the lunar surface while the Lunar Module was on the moon.

# Apollo missions

The Apollo 1 crew died in a fire during a launch rehearsal. Unmanned test flights paved the way for the other missions.

**Apollo 7**
In October 1968, Apollo 7 tested the redesigned spacecraft. The crew broadcast live TV images from space.

**Apollo 8**
The Apollo 8 crew was the first to fly to the moon, making 10 lunar orbits, in December 1968.

**Apollo 9**
In March 1969, the crew of Apollo 9 tested the Lunar Module while in orbit around the Earth.

**Apollo 10**
This final rehearsal for a landing descended to within 10 miles (16 km) of the moon's surface in May 1969.

**Apollo 12**
In November 1969, Apollo 12 landed close to the probe *Surveyor 3*, which had landed on the moon in 1966.

**Apollo 14**
Alan Shepard was the only astronaut from Project Mercury to set foot on the moon, in February 1971.

**Apollo 15**
This mission, in the summer of 1971, focused on science. Astronauts used an electric "Moon car" to explore.

**Apollo 16**
In April 1972, the Lunar Module landed in a highland region to study the moon's much older rocks.

**Apollo 17**
The final landing, in December 1972, included the only geologist (rock expert) to visit the moon.

# The Apollo space suit

The space suit worn by the Apollo astronauts was kind of like a spacecraft! It gave protection from tiny meteorites, the glare of the sun, and the vacuum of space. It also provided oxygen to breathe, removed carbon dioxide, and included a radio. Here is Neil Armstrong's space suit.

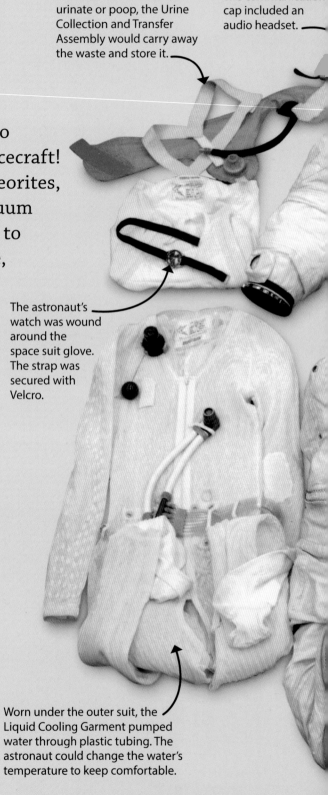

If an astronaut needed to urinate or poop, the Urine Collection and Transfer Assembly would carry away the waste and store it.

The communication cap included an audio headset.

The astronaut's watch was wound around the space suit glove. The strap was secured with Velcro.

Worn under the outer suit, the Liquid Cooling Garment pumped water through plastic tubing. The astronaut could change the water's temperature to keep comfortable.

### Joseph Kosmo

Starting at NASA in 1961, Joseph Kosmo worked on the space suit for Project Mercury. He was also involved with the design and testing of space suits for Gemini, Apollo, Skylab, and the space shuttle before retiring in 2011.

Joseph Kosmo checks a space suit.

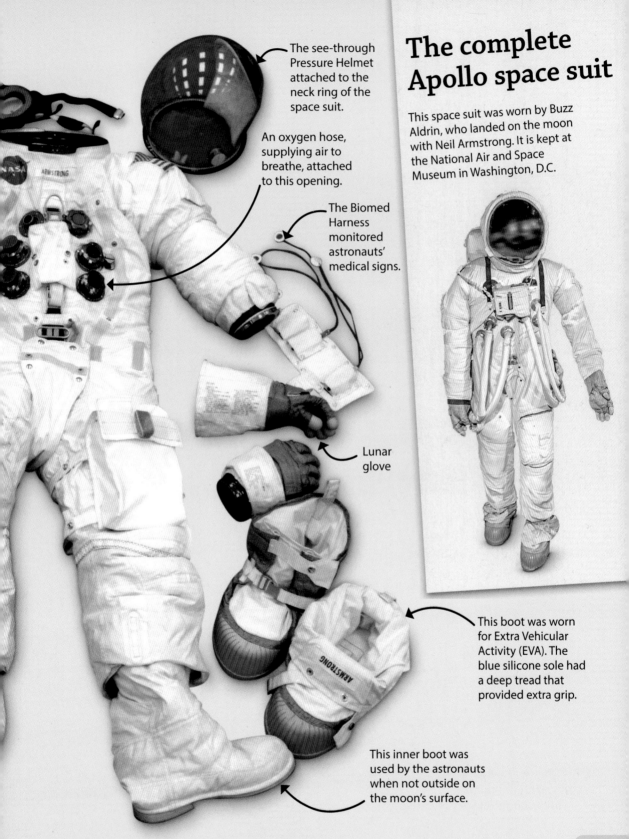

The see-through Pressure Helmet attached to the neck ring of the space suit.

An oxygen hose, supplying air to breathe, attached to this opening.

The Biomed Harness monitored astronauts' medical signs.

Lunar glove

# The complete Apollo space suit

This space suit was worn by Buzz Aldrin, who landed on the moon with Neil Armstrong. It is kept at the National Air and Space Museum in Washington, D.C.

This boot was worn for Extra Vehicular Activity (EVA). The blue silicone sole had a deep tread that provided extra grip.

This inner boot was used by the astronauts when not outside on the moon's surface.

# Space stations

A space station is a laboratory in space where astronauts stay for long periods of time, carrying out scientific experiments. Large space stations are assembled in space, and other spacecraft dock onto them to deliver crews of astronauts and supplies.

## International Space Station (ISS)

ISS crew members usually sta for expeditions of six month carrying out scientific researc Living in weightlessness causes muscles to weaken, so astronauts must exercise for two hours every day.

## FACT FILE

» **Launched:** September 29, 2011

» **Current status:** Mission complete. Re-entered April 2, 2018

» **Length:** 34 ft (10.5 m)

» **Crew:** 2 crews of 3 astronauts

## Tiangong-1

China launched Tiangong-1 ("Heavenly Palace") in 2011. It was visited by two crews in Shenzou spacecraft in 2012 and 2013. In 2018, after being shut down, the station burned up reentering the Earth's atmosphere.

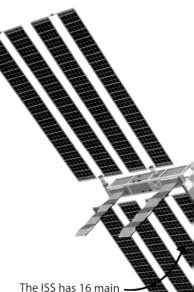

The ISS has 16 main modules that are powered by giant solar panels.

## Mir

The Soviet Mir ("Peace") space station was visited by 28 crews: 104 different people from 12 different countries. Mir gave us a lot of valuable information on what it's like to live in space for long periods.

## FACT FIL

» **Launched:** February 20, 1986

» **Current status:** Mission complete. Re-entered March 2 2001

» **Length:** 102 ft (31

» **Crew:** 28 crews of cosmonauts

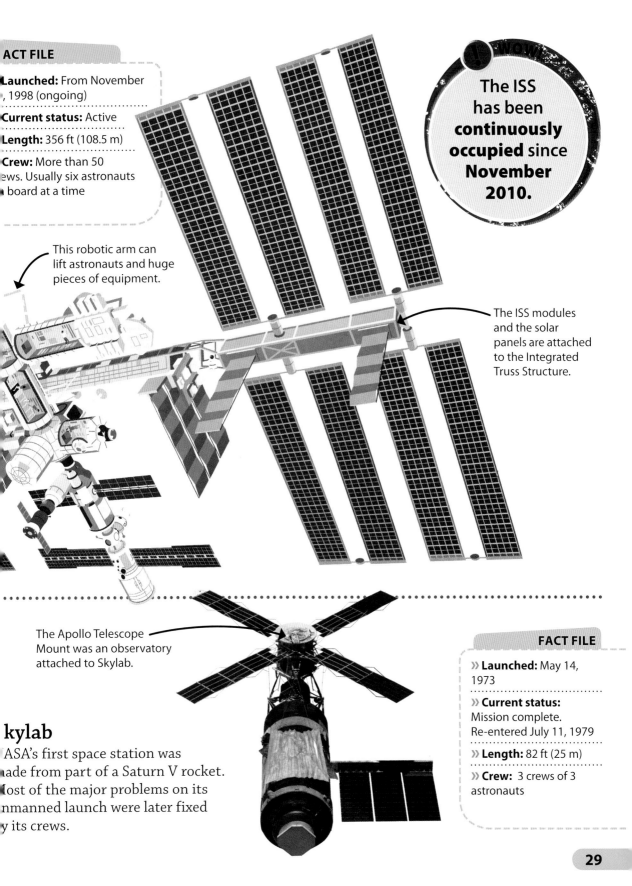

**Launched:** From November , 1998 (ongoing)

**Current status:** Active

**Length:** 356 ft (108.5 m)

**Crew:** More than 50 ews. Usually six astronauts board at a time

**WOW!**

The ISS has been **continuously occupied** since **November 2010.**

This robotic arm can lift astronauts and huge pieces of equipment.

The ISS modules and the solar panels are attached to the Integrated Truss Structure.

The Apollo Telescope Mount was an observatory attached to Skylab.

## kylab

ASA's first space station was ade from part of a Saturn V rocket. lost of the major problems on its nmanned launch were later fixed y its crews.

**FACT FILE**

» **Launched:** May 14, 1973

» **Current status:** Mission complete. Re-entered July 11, 1979

» **Length:** 82 ft (25 m)

» **Crew:** 3 crews of 3 astronauts

# Meet the expert

Dr. Shannon Lucid became an astronaut in 1979, after completing the NASA training program. She was the first woman to hold an international record for the most flight hours in orbit by any non-Russian. She retired from NASA in 2012.

**Q: What inspired you as a child?**

**A:** As a child I was intensely interested in the world around me. When I was in the fourth grade, I somehow learned that water was composed of hydrogen and oxygen. To me this was the most amazing thing. How could two gases make a liquid? How could anyone find out something like this? I was told that it was found out by chemists, so right then and there I decided to become a chemist. Also, I read about inventor Robert Goddard and the rockets he was testing. I thought I could be a chemist and work with rockets.

**Q: How did you become an astronaut?**

**A:** I had wanted to explore space as a child, before there was even a space program. Of course in the beginning of the human space program in America, it w open only to males. As soon as NASA said th were going to hire more astronauts, includin females, I applied and was accepted.

**Q: How many hours did you spend in spac and how many missions did you go on in total?**

**A:** I flew on five space shuttle missions for a total of 5,355 hours, or 223 days, in space.

**Q: What did lift-off into space feel like?**

**A:** For me there was a great feeling of relief as soon as I fe the solid rockets ignite becau that meant we were going somewhere and lift-off would not be scrubbed!

**Q: What was landing ba on Earth like?**

**A:** The primary emotion I had on reentry and landing was, "Oh my goodness, I fee so heavy! Do I really have to live the rest of my life feelin this heavy?"

**First female astronauts**
Shannon (second from the left) was among the first six women selected to be NASA astronauts.

**Q: What was a typical day like for you when you were in space?**

A: I flew on both short-duration shuttle flights and a long-duration flight of six months on the Russian space station Mir. The days on a short-duration flight were very different form the days on a long-duration flight. A short-duration flight was like running a sprint. You did not have to pace yourself, but put all your energy into dashing to the finish line. A long-duration flight is like a marathon. You have to pace yourself in order to be able to make it all the way to the finish line.

**Q: What did it feel like to look down on Earth from space?**

A: I spent as much free time as I could looking out the windows at the Earth. It always filled me with awe. I was impressed with how much of our Earth is water, and as we flew over land masses, I also thought about how much of the Earth I had never traveled to!

**Q: Did you do any experiments in space?**

A: Yes, I did many experiments in space. Many of the experiments were done to see how the human body changed in the space environment and how the human body adapted after returning to the Earth. I also did many experiments in physical science and biology.

**Q: Did you miss anything from Earth while you were living in space?**

A: Of course I missed my family.

On Mir, I also missed sunshine on my face and the wind in my hair.

**Q: What was the best thing about being an astronaut?**

**A:** The best thing about being an astronaut and flying in space was the people that you worked with.

**Q: What was the worst thing about being an astronaut?**

**A:** The worst thing about being an astronaut was the long wait to be assigned to a flight.

**Q: What would your advice for a future astronaut be?**

**A:** My advice is to study what you are really interested in and not to second-guess what will be criteria for getting hired as an astronaut, because things change. Just do the best that you can!

Shannon relaxing during her off-duty time in the shuttle Spacehab module.

# Living in space

People and objects—if not tied down—float in space. This state, called microgravity, makes things appear to be weightless. It creates daily life challenges for astronauts. Here are some of the experiences they have to deal with during their time in space.

## Cleaning up

Water floats around in balls in space. To keep clean, astronauts use washcloths and sponges. When washing hair, they use no-rinse shampoo.

## Keeping fit

In space, muscles and bones can weaken. To prevent this from happening, astronauts need to exercise two hours every day.

## Food

Food tastes different in space. Meals come in sealed packages and often need water added. Astronauts look forward to supplies of fresh fruit.

My food's floating!

## Working

The ISS is a microgravity research laboratory. Most of the astronauts' work involves various kinds of science. The results help us on Earth.

## Spacewalk

Sometimes astronauts go outside to install new equipment, to fit new sections onto the space station, or to make repairs. This work can take many hours.

## Fun and games

In their time off, astronauts can play musical instruments and read books. However, what they enjoy most is looking out of the windows at the Earth down below.

## Talking to loved ones

Astronauts have always been able to talk with their families by radio. The ISS has internet, and the astronauts can use email.

## Sleeping

Astronauts use sleeping bags. To stop themselves from floating around—and from bumping into things—when they are asleep, they can attach themselves to a wall.

# Experiments in space

Experiments done in space help us learn not only about the Earth and space, but also how the human body is affected by being in space. This is vital information if we want to travel to other planets, such as Mars.

## Putting out fire

More than 200 experiments on the ISS have shown that fire in space can begin at lower temperatures and require less oxygen. This research can have benefits for firefighting in space and also on the Earth.

Flames are ball-shaped in microgravity.

Microbes were tested on the ISS, rather than being brought back to the Earth to be looked at. This was a scientific first!

## Microbes

Microbes are tiny organisms, many of which are vital to human health. However, others can cause disease. In 2017, astronauts took samples of microbes found on the outside of the ISS! Luckily, they found all the samples to be harmless.

In 2014, **48** types of **microbes** from Earth were sent to the **ISS** to see how they **behave in space.**

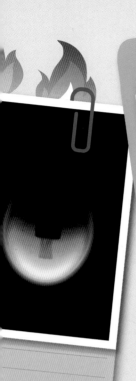

## Torso Rotation Experiment

On a Spacelab mission flown on the space shuttle in 1996, astronauts performed more than 40 experiments. In the Torso Rotation Experiment, Canadian astronaut Bob Thirsk looked at whether moving the body, or torso, to keep the head still in space caused motion sickness.

Bob Thirsk during the Torso Rotation Experiment.

These red lettuces were grown on the ISS.

## Growing food

Growing food in space will be essential in the future for long flights to places such as Mars. Fresh food can provide vitamins, and it reduces the need for packaged food. Astronauts on the ISS have eaten lettuce grown in space.

## Space lab

China launched Tiangong-2 ("Heavenly Palace"), a space laboratory, in September 2016. Two astronauts were on board the space lab for 30 days. They carried out scientific and technical tests on the effects of weightlessness on the human body.

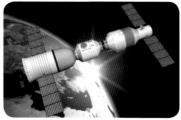

A Shenzou spacecraft docked to a Tiangong space station.

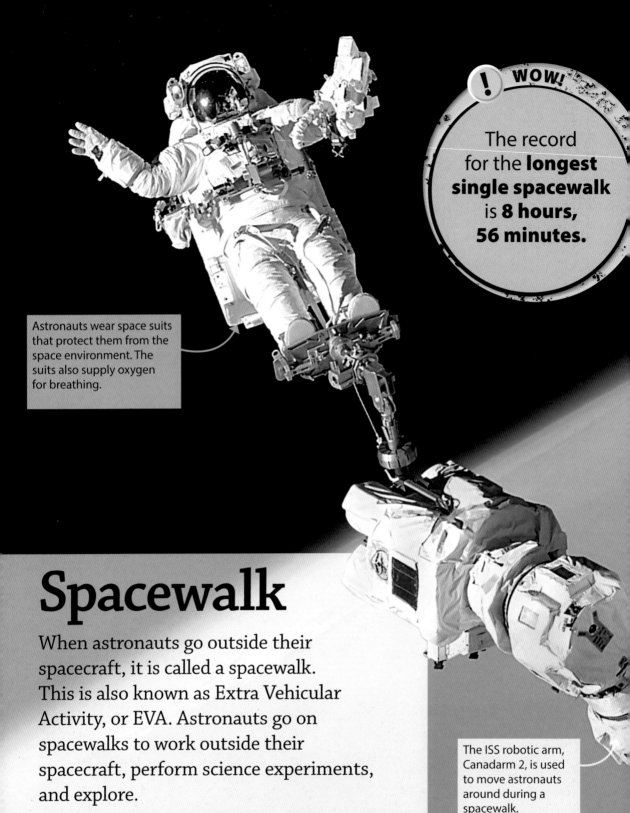

The record for the **longest single spacewalk** is **8 hours, 56 minutes.**

Astronauts wear space suits that protect them from the space environment. The suits also supply oxygen for breathing.

# Spacewalk

When astronauts go outside their spacecraft, it is called a spacewalk. This is also known as Extra Vehicular Activity, or EVA. Astronauts go on spacewalks to work outside their spacecraft, perform science experiments, and explore.

The ISS robotic arm, Canadarm 2, is used to move astronauts around during a spacewalk.

# Training for spacewalks

Before each mission, astronauts train for the job they need to perform in space. They spend hours learning how to handle space equipment.

Astronauts prepare for spacewalks by training underwater in a giant pool. By floating in water, astronauts feel like they are floating in space.

Virtual reality equipment is used to practice spacewalks. Astronauts wear a helmet with a video screen inside. It makes the astronauts feel as if they are really in space!

Training is carried out in the Partial Gravity Simulator (POGO) test area. Here, astronauts feel what it is like to move under gravity that is lower than that on Earth.

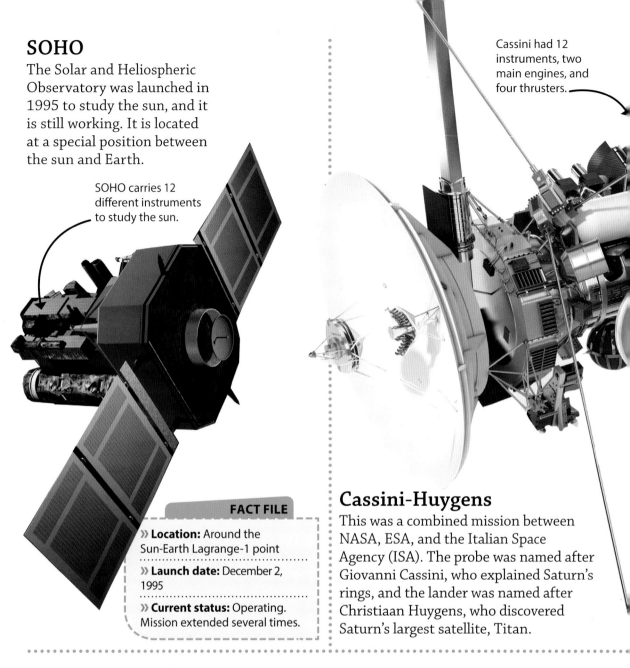

## SOHO

The Solar and Heliospheric Observatory was launched in 1995 to study the sun, and it is still working. It is located at a special position between the sun and Earth.

SOHO carries 12 different instruments to study the sun.

Cassini had 12 instruments, two main engines, and four thrusters.

### FACT FILE

» **Location:** Around the Sun-Earth Lagrange-1 point

» **Launch date:** December 2, 1995

» **Current status:** Operating. Mission extended several times.

## Cassini-Huygens

This was a combined mission between NASA, ESA, and the Italian Space Agency (ISA). The probe was named after Giovanni Cassini, who explained Saturn's rings, and the lander was named after Christiaan Huygens, who discovered Saturn's largest satellite, Titan.

# Searching space

Since Luna 1 in 1959, we have sent a wide range of unmanned spacecraft to investigate the moon, the sun, and the planets, as well as asteroids and comets. They have helped us learn far more than we could from ground instruments.

The Huygens probe became the first craft to land on Titan.

The 9 ft (2.7 m) heat shield protected Huygens during entry through Titan's atmosphere.

Rosetta contained science instruments and a high-resolution camera.

# Rosetta

A European Space Agency mission to study comet 67P/Churyumov-Gerasimenko, it became the first craft to orbit a comet, and the Philae lander was the first craft to land on one.

# New Horizons

This was the first spacecraft ever sent to Pluto. After its flyby in 2015, it was re-targeted to fly past object 2014 MU69, in the Kuiper Belt region, in January 2019.

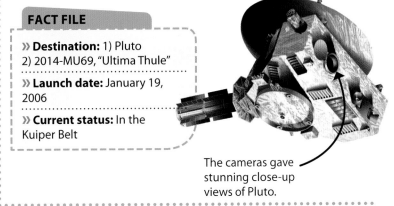

The cameras gave stunning close-up views of Pluto.

# Chang'e 2

A follow-on from China's Chang'e 1 lunar probe, it carried out research to help prepare for Chang'e 3's lander and lunar rover in 2013.

Chang'e 2 took lots of high quality images of the moon and the asteroid Toutatis.

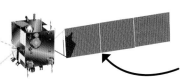

# Space telescopes

Telescopes in space allow us to see more of the universe than telescopes on the Earth. That's because the Earth's atmosphere blocks out a lot of the radiation, including gamma rays, X-rays, ultraviolet, infrared, and radio waves given off by stars and other distant objects.

## CHANDRA X-RAY OBSERVATORY

Named after the astrophysicist Subrahmanyan Chandrasekhar, this telescope was launched in 1999 from the space shuttle. It is much better at detecting X-ray sources than earlier telescopes.

## Spektr-R

Launched in 2011, Spektr-R is a radio telescope with a 33-ft (10-m) diameter antenna. By working together with observatories on the Earth, it can obtain extremely high levels of detail not possible before.

## KEPLER MISSION

This telescope focuses on a small area of our galaxy. It measures changes in starlight to detect planets orbiting other stars. So far it has found more than 2,000 planets.

# HUBBLE SPACE TELESCOPE

Hubble is named after the astronomer Edwin Hubble. It has given us many amazing pictures of the universe since its launch in 1990. Hubble orbits the Earth at a speed of 17,000 mph (27,350 kph).

## SPITZER SPACE TELESCOPE

This telescope was named after astronomer Lyman Spitzer who, in 1946, suggested putting telescopes in space. It was launched in 2003, and detects infrared, or heat radiation, given off by objects in space.

# Fermi gamma-ray space telescope

Launched in 2008, this telescope searches in all directions for explosions of light, called gamma-ray bursts, in distant galaxies; other high-energy sources; and evidence of dark matter.

**! WOW!**

The massive **James Webb Space Telescope (JWST)** is due to be launched in **2021**.

# Space base

This picture shows what a base on the moon could look like. So far, our explorations on the moon have lasted only three days, but future missions will last much longer. Mars is also being considered as a place to set up a base.

## Resources in space

The Apollo flights showed that moon soil contains oxygen (which could be used by humans to breathe), silicon (which could be used to make glass), and iron and aluminum (which could be used for construction). We have also discovered water frozen beneath the surface.

# Space shelters

Humans who want to live on the moon or Mars will have to learn to live with the harsh conditions, such as low temperatures and thin air.

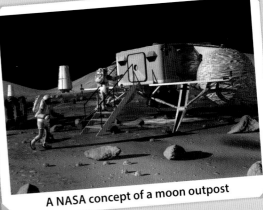

A NASA concept of a moon outpost

### Lunar outpost

When we return to the moon in the future, astronauts might use a shelter like this while exploring during a couple of weeks on the surface.

Astronauts on Mars might bury their habitats with local soil.

### Martian habitats

On the moon and Mars, people need protection from radiation (such as X-rays and high energy particles). One way could be to cover the habitats with soil, which would also shelter people from extreme temperatures.

# Exploring space

We explore space in many ways. We have unmanned craft such as satellites, space probes, and space telescopes. We also have manned spacecraft, and have been to the moon.

Roll a die and begin exploring.

**1** You are working on a rocket to take you to the moon. **Miss a turn!**

**2**

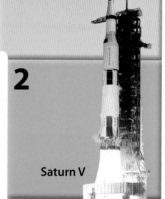

Saturn V

**3** **The first humans have landed on the moon! Move ahead 3 spaces.** Apollo 11 astronauts Neil Armstrong and Buzz Aldrin landed on the moon while Michael Collins orbited the moon, on July 20, 1969.

**4**

**9**

Viking 1

**8**

**7** Oh no! Your probe crashed. Go back one space!

**6**

Mariner

**5** **The first pictures of Mercury are taken! Roll the die again.** Space probe Mariner 10 was able to map about 45 percent of Mercury's surface before its final flyby on March 16, 1975

## TESS

The Transiting Exoplanet Survey Satellite (TESS) is a space telescope designed to search for exoplanets. These are planets outside of the solar system. At the time of launch in 2018, fewer than 4,000 exoplanets had been found. TESS is expected to discover more than 20,000.

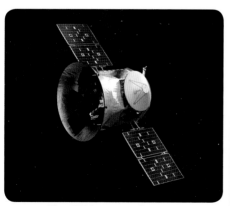

The TESS space telescope

**0** **First Mars landing! Move ahead one space.**
...king 1 became the ...rst spacecraft to ...uccessfully land on ...Mars on July 20, 1976.

**11**

Maat mons volcano, Venus

**12**

**13** **Your lander transmitted colored pictures! Move ahead 2 spaces.**
Venera 13 landed on March 1, 1982. It was the first lander to transmit color images from the surface of Venus.

**17** **Your probe uncovered ...ptune's secrets. ...ve ahead 2 spaces.**
...its flyby of Neptune in ...9, Voyager 2 confirmed ...r rings and six ...known moons.

**16** **Your probe discovered new moons! Roll the die again.**
Voyager 2 discovered 11 moons when it reached Uranus in 1986!

**15**
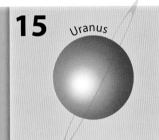
Uranus

**14** **You lost communication. Miss a turn and work on your probe!**

**8** **Your probe has launched ...e lander! Move ...ead 1 space.**
...ssini's lander Huygens ...scended onto Saturn's ...oon Titan in 2005.

**19**
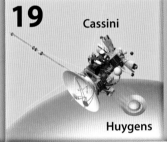
Cassini
Huygens

**20** **Your probe crashed into a small asteroid. You'll have to build it again. Move back 3 spaces and miss a turn!**

**21**

**25**

New Horizons

**24** **You've reached Pluto! Roll the die again.**
New Horizons spacecraft was the first ever to visit dwarf planet Pluto in July 2015.

**23**

Juno

**Your spacecraft has entered Jupiter's orbit! Move ahead 1 space.** **22**
NASA's spacecraft Juno entered orbit around Jupiter on July 5, 2016.

**6** **Successful landing on a comet! Move ...head 2 spaces.**
...osetta spacecraft's ...nder module, Philae, ...uccessfully landed ...n a comet on ...ovember 12, 2014.

**27**

Rosetta

# Congratulations! You've finished your voyage.
However, our exploration of space continues. Spacecraft are launched all the time, and we are planning to return to the moon and go to Mars!

**FINISH**

# Space tourism

In 2001, Dennis Tito became the first "space flight participant," or space tourist. Before then only astronauts and cosmonauts had flown into space, sent by the country they come from. Tito paid more than $20 million to spend a week on the ISS. He had to complete training before heading into space.

**KEY**

**1  Virgin Galactic** SpaceShipTwo will be released from a carrier aircraft, and then fire a rocket engine to reach space.

**2  Blue Origin** Started by the founder of Amazon, Jeff Bezos, Blue Origin is developing reusable spacecraft and launchers.

**3  ISS** This is currently the only place in orbit where people can stay. There are plans for space hotels.

**4  Space junk** One problem facing satellites and spacecraft is the amount of trash orbiting the Earth, from flecks of paint to leftover rocket stages. Hitting even a tiny item at high speeds can cause serious damage!

Virgin Galactic will fly its passengers to over 62 miles (100 km), giving them six minutes of weightlessness.

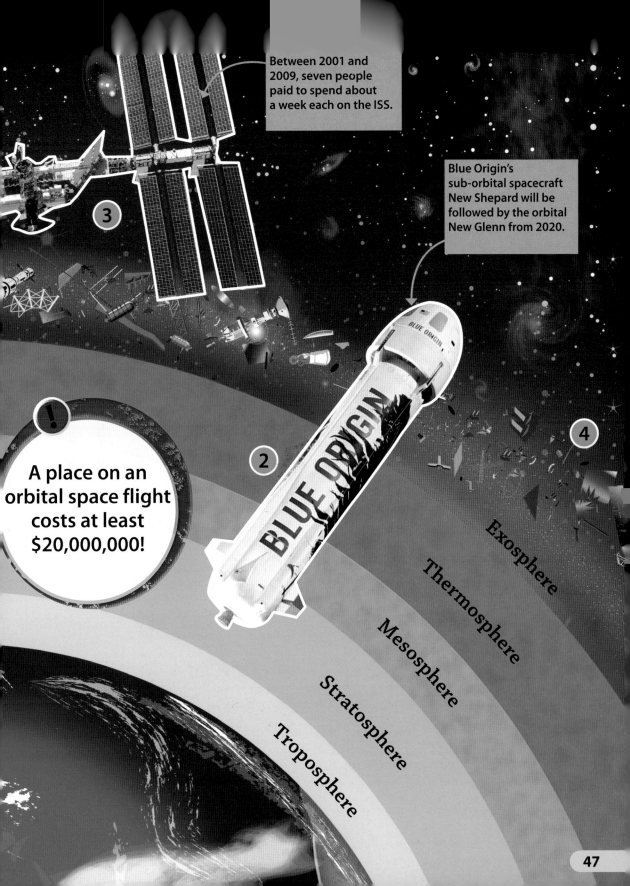

Between 2001 and 2009, seven people paid to spend about a week each on the ISS.

Blue Origin's sub-orbital spacecraft New Shepard will be followed by the orbital New Glenn from 2020.

③

④

②

!

A place on an orbital space flight costs at least $20,000,000!

Exosphere

Thermosphere

Mesosphere

Stratosphere

Troposphere

BLUE ORIGIN

## Fruit fly

The first animals in space were fruit flies launched in 1947 by the USA on a captured German V2 rocket. The flies were ejected and recovered.

**REALLY?**

In 1968, Russia sent **two tortoises** around the **moon** on **Zond 5.**

## Mouse

The first space mouse was launched in 1950 on a V2 rocket. In June 2018, SpaceX launched 20 mice to the ISS.

## Dog

In 1957, Russia launched the first living creature to orbit the Earth, a dog named Laika ("Barker"), but the spacecraft could not be recovered.

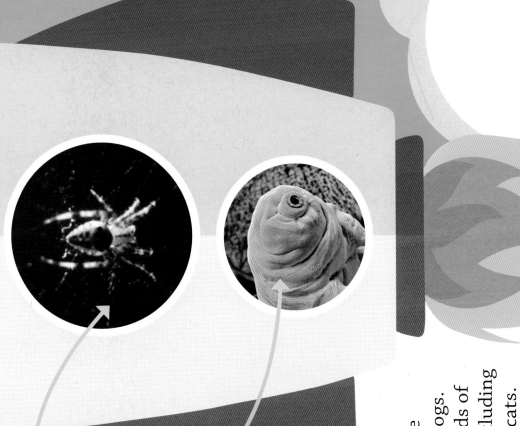

## Spider

In 1973, two spiders, Anita and Arabella, were taken to the Skylab space station to see if they could spin a web when weightless. (They could!)

## Tardigrade

In 2007, the European Space Agency's (ESA) FOTON-M3 mission carried some tardigrades, also known as water bears. They survived 10 days of exposure to open space.

# Animals in space

Before humans went into space, Russia and the USA sent animals to see if space was safe for living beings. Russia sent dogs. America sent chimpanzees. Now all kinds of animals have been flown into space, including newts, fish, frogs, rabbits, shrimp, and cats.

# Looking for life

One of our biggest questions as humans is, "Are we alone?" Is Earth the only planet in the universe that has life? We have found thousands of planets around other stars, and research suggests that many should have life, but we can't tell for sure.

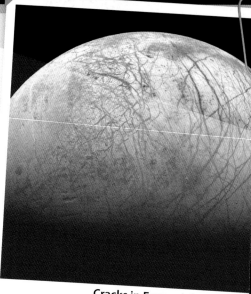

Cracks in Europa's ice

## Europa

One of the four main moons of Jupiter, Europa has a very smooth surface of ice. There could be liquid water below, which makes it possible that life could exist there.

Mars today is a desert world.

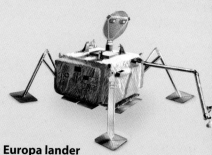

**Europa lander**
This is a lander that could search for life on Europa. It would need to drill through ice into the ocean to find anything!

## Life on Mars?

We have learned that Mars used to be warmer and wetter than it is now, so it might be possible that it had life in the past.

**Meteorite**
This meteorite was thought by people to contain bacteria from Mars. Scientists are not sure.

## Green Bank Telescope

This is the world's largest fully-steerable radio telescope. Since 2016 it has been part of the "Breakthrough Listen project," which is expected to last 10 years. It is searching for possible signals from other worlds.

**The GBT in West Virginia**

**! WOW!**

The diameter of GBT's telescope is **328 ft** (100 m).

**The Arecibo Observatory in Puerto Rico**

# The Arecibo Signal

In 1974, the Arecibo Observatory telescope was upgraded, and the staff sent a message out into the universe. A receiver can decode it and produce the diagram shown here.

**The decoded message**
It was sent in binary code. Colors have been added to make sections stand out.

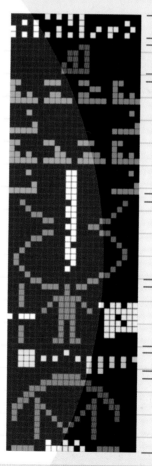

Number 1–10 (White).

Atomic numbers for hydrogen, carbon, nitrogen, oxygen, and phosphorus (Purple).

Chemical components of DNA (Green).

Information on human DNA (White) and a diagram of the double helix (Blue).

A human figure (Red). Average height (Blue/White). Human population (White).

The solar system, indicating the Earth (Yellow).

The Arecibo radio telescope (Purple). Size of telescope (Blue/White).

# Rovers

Rovers are vehicles designed to travel across the surface of a planet or moon. They can operate for longer than astronauts, and in places that could be dangerous for humans, but they need to be programmed and cannot be repaired.

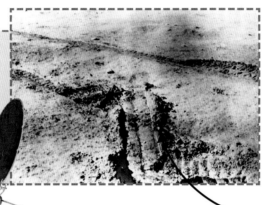

## Lunokhod 1 and 2

The Soviet Union's Lunokhod 1 drove only 6.5 miles (10.54 km) over 321 days (11 lunar days), but Lunokhod 2 lasted for four months, covering 24.† miles (39 km).

Lunokhod's tracks on the lunar surface.

The astronauts are more than 3.1 miles (5 km) away from the Lunar Module.

## Lunar Roving Vehicle

The last three Apollo missions each carried a Lunar Roving Vehicle (LRV)—an electric car. They let the astronauts travel across the moon, exploring a larger area and gathering a wider range of samples.

The LRVs were powered by two batteries.

Sojourner's view toward the Twin Peaks on Mars.

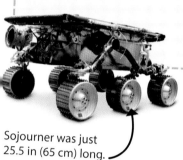

Sojourner was just 25.5 in (65 cm) long.

## Sojourner

NASA's Mars Pathfinder carried a small rover, called Sojourner. Although it only explored Mars for three months, traveling just 328 ft (100 m), it showed that it was possible to use a rover on Mars. Later rovers were much larger.

View of the base of Mount Sharp

Its robotic arm holds five instruments.

## uriosity

ASA's fourth Mars rover, the Mars Science Laboratory, known as Curiosity. It's the size of a small car and is clear-powered, unlike previous craft that relied on lar panels to charge batteries.

### Spacecraft or rocket engineer
These people design and build satellites, space probes, planetary rovers, and manned spacecraft. They make all the parts and then assemble them.

### Science officer
The ISS is a science laboratory in space. You could design experiments, and even perform them on board.

# Space careers

Activity in space affects almost all of us on a daily basis, whether by weather forecasting, satellite navigation (satnav) systems in cars, satellite TV, and much more. Apart from working in space, there are all kinds of space-related careers you could have in lots of different locations.

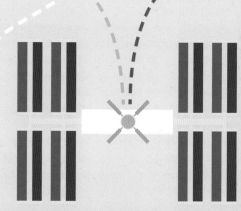

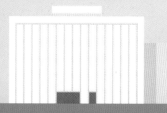

**Mission control center**
This is where space flights are managed and monitored, usually all the way from lift-off to landing. One of the many jobs based here is that of a flight controller.

**ISS**
Thousands of people have jobs linked with the ISS. There are astronauts living and working on board the ISS, but there are also people doing a variety of jobs that support these astronauts.

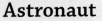

## Flight controller

The flight controllers monitor different parts of space missions and provide assistance during a flight. There are also lots of support roles.

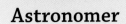

## Astronaut

An astronaut has the role of a pilot, a mission commander, or a payload specialist (an astronaut who handles equipment and conduct experiments). All roles are important, and they work together closely.

## Astronomer

Astronomers study planets, stars, and galaxies. They make discoveries, whether through using telescopes on the Earth or in space.

**Spacecraft**
It takes a lot of people with different skills to design and build a spacecraft or rocket.

**Observatory**
Although we have put telescopes in space, the ones on the Earth are much bigger. There are numerous jobs involved in the running of an observatory.

**Launch center**
This is where rockets are assembled and the spacecraft or space probes are fitted. Lots of different jobs are needed for lift-off!

# Future of space travel

In the immediate future, humans will continue to work on the ISS. Plans are in place to send astronauts back to the moon and then on to Mars. Unmanned craft will continue to explore the solar system and look out to the rest of the universe. There is so much we've yet to discover.

## Planned missions

OSIRIS-Rex is a NASA mission launched in 2016. It's due to bring back samples from an asteroid in 2023. NASA sent InSight in 2018. It is heading to Mars to drill below the ground. ESA and NASA will launch craft to Mars in 2020.

The satellite will send information to Earth from the rover and the lander.

**Chang'e 4**
Chang'e 4 was planned as the first craft to land on the far side of the moon. A separate communications satellite will relay signals from the lander.

## Humans in space

In 2021, ESA and NASA are due to launch up to four astronauts in a manned Orion mission. This will be the first time humans have left low orbit since 1972. Virgin Galactic plans to fly hundreds of space tourists, and Elon Musk (the founder of SpaceX) wants to send large numbers of people to the moon and to Mars.

The ESA-NASA Orion spacecraft

**Europa probe**
Jupiter's moon, Europa, is covered in ice. It may have a liquid water ocean underneath, where life might exist.

Its huge mirror is five times as big as Hubble's.

Robonaut 2 does dangerous EVA jobs in place of an astronaut.

**James Webb Space Telescope (JWST)**
A successor to the Hubble Space Telescope (HST), JWST will operate in infrared wavelengths, allowing it to detect objects too old and distant for Hubble to observe.

**Robotic explorers**
Robonaut 2 is being tested on the ISS, and full robotic explorers may help us explore space, going to distant places and locations too dangerous for humans.

# Facts and figures

Space is filled with unknown things and many surprises. Here are some weird and wonderful facts about space and space travel that you can impress your friends with.

Scientists believe that **HUMANS** could actually be **exploring Mars** by **2040**.

**HUMANS** have been **traveling** into space since **1961.**

**280**

280 lb

A space suit weighs approximately 280 lb (127 kg)—without the astronaut. It takes between 30–45 minutes to put it on.

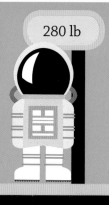

**400**

We've been using telescopes for more than 400 years to look into space.

The total cost of the entire **Apollo program** was **$25.4 billion**. In today's money, that's around **$150 billion**.

**Bruce McCandless** was the first astronaut to float untethered from a spacecraft during an EVA.

In **2001**, a pizza company **"DELIVERED" a pizza** by rocket **to astronauts** on board the ISS.

# 50

There are about 50 launch sites around the Earth.

# 1,000

To become a pilot-astronaut, the candidate must have completed 1,000 hours of flying time in a jet aircraft.

# Glossary

Here are the meanings of words that are good to know when learning about space travel.

**Arecibo message** Radio message broadcast into space by the Arecibo Observatory giving information about humans and the Earth, in the hope it might reach intelligent alien life

**asteroid** Rocky object smaller than a planet. Most asteroids orbit the sun between Mars and Jupiter

**astronaut** Space traveler; someone who is trained to take part in a space flight

**astrophysicist** Someone who studies the nature of stars and galaxies

**atmosphere** Layers of gases surrounding a planet, moon, or star

**comet** Icy object orbiting a star. When it gets closer to the star, a tail may form

**dark matter** Invisible material believed to exist in space. Astrophysicists think that dark matter makes up 80 percent of material in the universe

**dwarf planet** Any of five objects, including Pluto, in our solar system that are smaller than the eight main planets

**Earth** Third planet from the sun; the home of the human race and where all known life exists

**galaxy** Huge collection of stars, from a few hundred million up to thousands of billions of stars

**gravity** Force that causes all things to be attracted to others. It explains why apples fall to the ground and why planets orbit the sun

**infrared** Radiation with wavelengths longer than that of visible light. Infrared astronomy can show objects from the early period of the universe

**laboratory** Place where scientific experiments are performed

**lunar** Belonging to the moo[n]

**Mars** Fourth planet from the sun and target of many spacecraft as part of our search for life elsewhere

**matter** In general terms, anything that has mass and takes up some space

**meteor** Object that burns u[p] when passing at high speed through the atmosphere. Usually about the size of a grain of sand, meteors are known as "shooting stars"

**Milky Way** Spiral galaxy tha[t] contains our solar system

**module** Unit of a spacecraft

**moon** Natural satellite of a planet

**nebula** Cloud of gas and du[st] in space

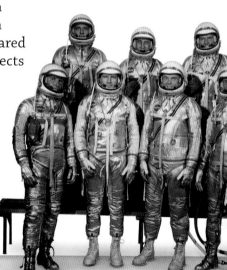

**The Project Mercury astronauts**

**rbit** Path of an object ound another, such as planet around a star

**rbiter** Part of the space uttle that carried cargo nd crew members into orbit

**lanet** Round object, such Mars, Venus, or Jupiter, at orbits the sun

**robe** Unmanned spacecraft esigned to study objects in pace and send information ack to the Earth

**over** Wheeled vehicle, ther manned or unmanned, sed to explore the surface f a planet or other body

**atellite** Object that rbits another body, such a planet around a star r a spacecraft around e Earth

**olar** Belonging to the sun

**olar system** sun and the ther objects that orbit it

**pace** Also known as outer space," the region eyond the Earth's tmosphere between ther objects

**pacecraft** Vehicle, either nanned or unmanned, esigned to fly in space

**space flight** Voyage by a spacecraft into space above the Earth or deeper into space

**Space Race** Rival space-related activities between the Soviet Union and the United States. It started with the launch of Sputnik 1 and resulted in the first humans on the moon

**spaceplane** Vehicle designed to be launched into space and land on a runway, to be reused

**space probe** Spacecraft that does not orbit the Earth but is sent to explore deep space or other planets

**space shuttle** General term for the Space Transportation System, consisting of the Space Shuttle Orbiter, its Solid Rocket Boosters, and External Tank

**space suit** Protective clothing worn by space travelers to provide oxygen and a radio, and protection from the environment of space

**spacewalk** Also called extravehicular activity (EVA), any activity in which an astronaut goes outside a spacecraft, such as to make repairs or walk on the moon's surface

Arecibo message

**stage** Section of a rocket

**star** Huge ball of gas generating light and heat

**sun** Star at the center of our solar system. The Earth and other planets orbit the sun

**telescope** Instrument for looking at distant objects

**ultraviolet** Radiation with wavelengths shorter than that of visible light

**universe** Everything in space, including all the stars, nebulae, and galaxies

**weightlessness** Lack of weight in space that allows people and objects to float

# Index

## A

Aldrin, Edwin "Buzz" 8, 10, 24, 27
Apollo missions 8, 19, 24–27, 42, 52, 59
Arecibo message 51
Aristotle 6
Armstrong, Neil 8, 10, 24, 26–27
asteroids 5, 56
astronauts 8–9, 24–27, 30–31, 32–37, 55, 59
astronomers 6–7, 55

## B

Bezos, Jeff 46
biomedical engineers 23
Blue Origin 46, 47
Boeing X-37B 20–21

## C

careers, space 54–55
Cassini 38–39
Cat's Paw nebula 4
Chandra X-ray Observatory 40
Chandrayaan-1 13
Chang'e spacecraft 39, 56
Chinese National Space Administration (CNSA) 13, 18, 28, 39, 56
comets 5, 39
communications 23, 33
Copernicus, Nicolaus 7
cosmonauts 8–9
Curiosity 53

## D

dark matter 41

docking 16

## E

Earth 6, 7
engineers 54
Europa 50, 57
European Space Agency (ESA) 12, 38, 39, 56, 57
EVA (Extra-Vehicular Activity) 8, 23, 33, 36, 59
experiments 32, 34–35
Explorer 1 11

## F

Falcon rocket 18
Fermi gamma-ray space telescope 41
fire 34
fitness 32
flight controllers 55
flight directors 23
flight surgeons 23
food 32, 35

## G

Gagarin, Yuri 8, 11
Gaia 12
galaxies 4
Galilei, Galileo 7
Gemini spacecraft 11
Glenn, John 11
Green Bank Telescope 51

## H

H-IIA rocket 13
Hubble Space Telescope 41, 57
Huygens lander 38–39

## I

Indian Space Research Organisation (ISRO) 13, 19
InSight 12, 56
International Space Station (ISS) 9, 16, 28–29, 32–35, 36, 46–47, 54, 56
Italian Space Agency (ISA) 38

## J

James Webb Space Telescope 41, 57
Japan Aerospace Exploration Agency (JAXA) 13
Johnson Space Center 22–23
Jupiter 7, 50, 57

## K

Kennedy, John F 8, 10–11, 24
Kepler mission 40
Knight, William 21
Kosmo, Joe 26
Kuiper Belt 39

## L

Laika 48
launch sites 55, 59
leisure activities 33
Leonov, Alexei 8
life 50–51
lift-off 16
Lobster nebula 4
Long March 2F 18
Lucid, Shannon 30–31
Luna 3 11
Lunar Roving Vehicle (LVR) 52
Lunokhod 1 and 2 52

cCandless, Bruce 59
ars 12, 13, 42, 43, 50, 53, 56,
  57, 58
ars Pathfinder 53
ercury 7 10
eteorites 50
eteors 5
icrobes 34
ilky Way 4
ir 9, 16, 28, 31
ission control 13, 22–23, 54
oon 6, 7, 13
oon exploration 38, 39,
  2–43, 52, 56, 57
oon landings 8, 10, 24–25
oons 5, 7, 50, 57
usk, Elon 57

ASA 12, 16, 29, 30, 38, 53, 57
ebulae 4
ew Horizons 39
orth American X-15 20–21

servatories 12, 55
rbiters 14, 15, 16–17
rion Spacecraft 57
SIRIS-Rex 56
xygen 26, 34, 36, 42

adalka, Gennady 9
artial Gravity Simulator (PGS)
  37
hilae lander 39
anets 5
uto 39
SLV (Polar Satellite Launch
  Vehicle) 19
tolemy 6

**R**
radiation 43
radio telescopes 51
reentry 17
Robonaut-2 57
rockets 13, 18–19, 54
Rosetta 39
rovers 52–53
Russian space agency
  (Roscosmos) 13

**S**
Sänger, Eugen 20
satellites 11, 12, 13, 54
Saturn 38
Saturn V rocket 19
science officers 54
shelters, space 43
Shepard, Alan 11
Skylab 29
Skylon 20–21
sleep 33
SOHO (Solar and Heliospheric
  Observatory) 38
Sojourner 53
solar system 4, 5
Soyuz spacecraft 19
space 4–5
space agencies 12–13
space bases 42–43
space junk 46
space probes 12, 13, 38–39
space programs 12–13,
  56–57
Space Race 8, 10–11
space shuttle 14–17, 30
space stations 28–29, 31
space telescopes 13, 40–41, 44,
  57
space tourism 46–47, 57
spacecraft communicators 23
spaceplanes 20–21

SpaceShipOne 20–21
SpaceShipTwo 21, 46
space suits 26–27, 36, 58
spacewalks 8, 23, 33, 36–37, 59
Spektr-R 40
Spitzer Space Telescope 41
Sputnik 1 10–11
stars 4
sun 5, 6, 7, 38

**T**
telescopes 7, 40–41, 51, 55, 57,
  58
temperatures 26, 43
Tereshkova, Valentina 9
TESS (Transiting Exoplanet
  Survey Satellite) 44
Tiangong spacecraft 28, 35
Titan 38, 39
Tito, Dennis 46
training 37, 59

**U**
underwater training 37
universe 4, 6, 56

**V**
Virgin Galactic 46, 57
virtual reality 37
Vostok 1 8, 11

**W**
Walker, Joe 20
washing 32
water 42, 50, 57
weightlessness 32, 35, 46
White, Ed 11
Whitson, Peggy 9

**Y**
Yang Liwel 13

# Acknowledgments

**The publisher would like to thank the following people for their assistance in the preparation of this book:** Caroline Bingham, Katie Lawrence, and Jack Shelton for proofreading, Marie Greenwood and Jolyon Goddard for editorial assistance, Emma Hobson for design assistance, Helen Peters for compiling the index, Dan Crisp for illustrations. The publishers would also like to thank Dr. Shannon Lucid for the "Meet the expert" interview.

The publisher would like to thank the following for their kind permission to reproduce their photographs:

(Key: a-above; b-below/bottom; c-center; f-far; l-left; r-right; t-top)

**2 NASA:** (br); Jerry Woodfill (bl). **3 Dorling Kindersley:** Andy Crawford (tr). **Dreamstime. com:** Yael Weiss (bc/Magnifying glass). **Getty Images:** QAI Publishing / UIG (cb). **NASA:** Bill Ingalls (br); Desiree Stover (bl); JSC / Stanford University (bc). **4-5 ESA / Hubble:** NASA. **4 ESO:** (crb). **5 123RF.com:** qq47182080 (crb). **Dreamstime.com:** Mozzyb (clb); Levgenii Tryfonov / Trifff (tr). **6-7 Dreamstime.com:** Andreykuzmin (Background). **6 iStockphoto. com:** ZU_09 (bl); Wynnter (r). **7 Getty Images:** Popperfoto (br); Time Life Pictures / Mansell / The LIFE Picture Collection (cl). **8-9 123RF. com:** apostrophe. **ESO:** J. Emerson / VISTA. Acknowledgment: Cambridge Astronomical Survey Unit (Nebula). **8 Alamy Stock Photo:** SPUTNIK (tr). **Getty Images:** Sovfoto / UIG (clb). **NASA:** (crb). **9 Alamy Stock Photo:** SPUTNIK (tl). **NASA:** (cr); JSC (clb). **10 NASA:** (cl, bl, tr). **10-11 NASA:** (bc). **11 NASA:** (tc, cl, br). **12 ESA:** ATG medialab; background: ESO / S. Brunier (c). **NASA:** JPL-Caltech (bl). **13 Getty Images:** Pallava Bagla / Corbis (bc); Sergei Fadeichev\TASS (tl); VCG (cra); The Asahi Shimbun (br). **14 NASA:** (ca, clb). **14-15 NASA:** (t). **15 NASA:** (ca, b). **16-17 Getty Images:** Mark Wilson. **16 Getty Images:** Stan Honda / AFP (tc). **NASA:** (bc). **The National Archives of the UK:** National Archives photo no. 80-G-32500 (cla). **17 NASA:** (bc). **18 Getty Images:** Red Huber / Orlando Sentinel / TNS (l); VCG (r). **19 Alamy Stock Photo:** Dinodia Photos (l). **NASA:** (tc); Bill Ingalls (r). **20 Alamy Stock Photo:** Keystone Pictures USA / ZUMAPRESS (bl). **20-21 Getty Images:** Scaled Composites (ca). **NASA:** (t); MSFC (cb). **Reaction Engines Limited:** (b). **22-23 NASA. 24-25 NASA. 25 Dorling Kindersley:** Dave Shayler / Astro Info Service Ltd (ca, ca/Apollo 8, c, c/Apollo 10, c/Apollo 12, cb, cb/Apollo 15, bc, bc/Apollo 17). **26 NASA:** Bill Stafford (bl). **26-27 NASA. 27 Alamy Stock Photo:** Andy Morton (cr). **28 Avalon:** Liu Chan (cl). **Getty Images:** NASA (bc). **29 NASA:** (bc). **30 NASA:** (bc); Kim Shiflett (tr). **31 NASA:** (br). **32 ESA:** NASA (br). **Getty Images:** NASA / Roger Ressmeyer / Corbis / VCG (cb). **NASA:** (cl, cra). **33 NASA:** (t, cl, r); Bill Ingalls (bl). **34 NASA:** JPL (cb). **34-35 NASA. 35 Alamy Stock Photo:** Keystone Pictures USA (tr); Xinhua (crb). **NASA:** (cb). **36-37 NASA. 37 NASA:** (c, crb, bc). **38 NASA:** (l). **39 NASA:** Johns Hopkins University Applied Physics Laboratory / Southwest Research Institute (crb); JPL (t). **40 123RF.com:** Pere Sanz (c). **Fotolia:** eevl (b/ Spiral galaxy). **NASA:** (tr, tr/Galaxy); Ames / JPL-Caltech / T Pyle (b). **41 Dorling Kindersley:** Andy Crawford (cl/Telescope). **ESA / Hubble:** NASA (cl). **Fotolia:** dundanim (b/Earth). **NASA:** JPL (tr); Sonoma State University / Aurore Simonnet (b). **42-43 NASA:** Pat Rawlings, (SAIC). Technical concepts for NASA's Exploration Office, Johnson Space Center (JSC). **43 Foster + Partners:** (crb). **NASA:** (cra). **44 Dorling Kindersley:** Stephen Oliver (ca). **Getty Images:** SSPL (crb). **NASA:** (bc, tr, c); Goddard (bl). **45 Getty Images:** QAI Publishing / UIG (c). **NASA:** Johns Hopkins University Applied Physics Laboratory / Southwest Research Institute (clb); JPL (tc, bc); JPL-Caltech (cb). **46-47 NASA:** (t). **46 Getty Images:** Mark Greenberg / Virgin Galactic (cr). **47 Blue Origin:** (c). **48 Dorling Kindersley:** Liberty's Owl, Raptor and Reptile Centre, Hampshire, UK (cra). **Dreamstime.com:** Jahoo (ca). **48-49 Science Photo Library:** Sputnik (ca). **49 Depositphotos Inc:** Rukanoga (ca/ Tardigrade). **NASA:** JSC (ca). **50-51 Dreamstime.com:** Geopappas (Paper clip). **50 Dreamstime.com:** Yael Weiss (br/ Magnifying glass). **NASA:** JPL-Caltech / SETI Institute (tr); Greg Shirah (clb); JPL-Caltech (crb); JSC / Stanford University (br). **51 Dreamstime.com:** Dennis Van De Water (clb). **Getty Images:** Andrew Caballero-Reynolds / AFP (tc). **52 Getty Images:** Sovfoto / UIG (c). **NASA:** Eugene Cernan (cb). **52-53 Dreamstime.com:** Amabrao (Border); Jason Winter / Eyematrix (Tyre). **53 Getty Images:** AFP (cra). **NASA:** JPL-Caltech / MSSS (clb); Jerry Woodfill (cla); JPL-Caltech (crb). **54 NASA:** (tl, cra). **55 NASA:** Tony Landis (tr); (cla, c). **56-57 NASA:** JPL-Caltech. **57 NASA:** (tr, br); Desiree Stover (clb). **58-59 ESA / Hubble:** NASA (t). **58 ESA / Hubble:** NASA (br). **59 Dreamstime.com:** Scol22 (tr). **NASA:** (tl, cr); Norman Kuring, NASA's Ocean Biology Processing Group. Story by Kathryn Hansen and Pola Lem (cr/Blacksea); Bill Ingalls (bl). **60 NASA:** (br). **64 Dreamstime.com:** Mozzyb (tl

**Endpaper images:** *Front:* **Alamy Stock Photo:** Pictorial Press Ltd ftl; **NASA:** tc, clb, bc, ca, GSFC fcrb, JPL-Caltech bc (Cassini), fcr; *Back:* **Alamy Stock Photo:** SPUTNIK cla; **NASA:** bl, ca, bc, bc (Floating Free), cra, br.

**Cover images:** *Front:* **Dorling Kindersley:** Dave Shayler / Astro Info Service Ltd cra; **NASA:** c; **Science Photo Library:** NASA cr; *Back:* **Dreamstime.com:** Scol22 cla; **NASA:** JPL-Caltech bl; **Science Photo Library:** SPUTNIK cr; *Spine:* **Dreamstime.com:** Konstantin Shaklein / 3dsculptor cb; *Front Flap:* **Dorling Kindersley:** Bob Gathany cla/ (Lunar module), Dave Shayler / Astro Info Service Ltd cb; **NASA:** ca, ca/ (Atlantis), c, cr, bc tl/ (2), br/ (2), Bill Ingalls clb/ (2), Johns Hopkins University Applied Physics Laboratory / Southwest Research Institute cla, Jerry Woodfill bc; *Back Flap:* **NASA:** cb, Hubble Heritage Team, ESA cb/ (Galaxy).

All other images © Dorling Kindersley
For further information see:
www.dkimages.com

## My Findout facts:

# Evolution of space suits

## SK-1 pressure space suit, 1961

This space suit was worn by Yuri Gagarin when he became the first person in space, and by other cosmonauts on Vostok missions.

The suit had a mirror in the sleeve. This helped the cosmonaut locate switches that were hard to see.

## Project Mercury space suit, 1961

The helmet could be removed once in orbit.

The space suit had 13 zippers, which ensured a good fit.

America's first astronauts flew in the one-man Mercury spacecraft. Their space suit was a modified version of the Navy Mark IV pressure suit used by fighter pilots.

## Project Gemini space suit, 1965

The helmet included earphones and microphones.

Extra layers were added for working outside the spacecraft.

The space suit for the two-man Gemini missions was based on the high-altitude pressure suit worn by pilots of the X-15 rocket plane.

## Apollo 11 space suit, 1969

This famous photo shows Buzz Aldrin wearing the A7L space suit. When worn on the moon, it included a Portable Life Support System "backpack."

Special lunar overshoes provided extra grip on the moon's surface.